The digital marketing manual for accountants

PracticeWeb

Who is PracticeWeb?

PracticeWeb is a digital marketing agency based in Bristol. Set up in 1999, our ethos is about putting accountants and their clients at the centre of everything we do.

We recognise every accounting firm is different, with its own characteristics, working with all kinds of customers. That's why we're committed to helping ambitious firms differentiate themselves in a crowded marketplace, to connect with the right prospects, and to achieve their business and marketing goals.

practiceweb.co.uk

Table of contents

About this manual

Our clients are expert accountants but tend to have a lot of questions about marketing. How often should I post on LinkedIn? Why isn't my firm ranking in Google results? How can I generate more leads, of the right type?

This book, two years in the making, takes every answer we've ever given, every bit of expertise we have, and boils it down into an easy-to-follow practical guide.

It sets out our tried-and-tested method for creating an effective marketing strategy for your accountancy practice, starting with the powerful concept of the ideal client. There are also practical exercises to help you package and price your services; to review your existing marketing performance; and to build a marketing plan that will achieve results.

We want to give firm owners and partners the information and education they need to become confident in:

- buying marketing services
- defining marketing strategy
- managing marketers
- executing their plan and
- measuring return on investment.

Some of you will want to sit down and read the book from cover to cover. Others will find it more useful to dip in as and when they have specific questions about particular aspects of the marketing process. In the long term, we hope you'll all keep this book handy, refer to it and share it with your peers and colleagues.

The PracticeWeb team

Chapter 1

Why marketing matters

In this chapter

You will learn:
What's so difficult about marketing? Do accountancy firms need marketing? Where do we start?
30 min read.

If you're reading this book, we're going to assume you're already a believer in the power of marketing. If not, this should convince you to read on – at least a little further. More likely, though, is that you find yourself dealing with sceptical colleagues, in which case, we hope this gives you the ammunition you need to have meaningful conversations that move things forward.

What's so difficult about marketing?

Marketing can be a challenge for accountants, for various reasons.

First, there's the sheer amount of noise in the market. There are agencies, experts and gurus advocating all sorts of approaches, from social media pyramid schemes to – believe it or not – printed leaflets through the door.

Then there's the traditional tension between accountancy and creativity. Some accountants have a knack for brand and marketing strategy – they get graphic design and writing, they talk the talk. But most will admit that it's not where their interest or expertise lies.

Unfortunately, that can make them vulnerable to, for want of a better word, cowboys. Over the years, we've spent plenty of time unpicking the damage done by unscrupulous agencies who promised the earth, cheap and fast, only to do more damage than good.

Another challenge is the pace at which marketing moves. Search algorithms get updated. New social media services are launched, evolve or fizzle out. User expectations change. Novelty fades. And fashion is fickle – colours and fonts, however carefully chosen, will inevitably start to look dated after only a few years.

The biggest problem, though, is perhaps the priority marketing is given in many firms. Typically, when times are good, people are relatively happy to spend their surplus budget on marketing. When things feel tight, on the other hand, marketing spend is often the first thing that gets frozen or cut. We saw some of this in 2020 as the economic impact of the coronavirus pandemic began to bite.

That instinctive low priority given to marketing can be pretty frustrating if you're the accountancy firm partner who has taken responsibility for marketing. Even at the best of times, it can be a challenge to get fellow partners and managers to carve out time for marketing activity (which they find difficult and perhaps don't enjoy) when they could be undertaking billable client work – which is very much in their comfort zone.

All of that is why measuring return on investment (ROI) for marketing spend is so important. For example, if you spend a certain amount per month on search engine optimisation, you'll want to know that there's a corresponding uplift in conversions via the website. If you can see the difference marketing is making to your firm's income and long-term viability, the case to keep investing makes itself.

From the agency perspective, measuring ROI is important because it builds trust. Marketing can and should be as much science as art, especially in the digital age when everything can easily be tracked, monitored and measured.

Do accountancy firms need marketing?

Marketing is vital for the modern accountancy firm. To put it bluntly, your practice needs to make money, which means it needs clients, which means leads, which means marketing.

A handful of lucky accountants get plenty of business through referrals – although even that is a form of marketing. The rest of them are competing for the attention of potential clients.

That competition might include the ten other accountancy firms in town, big national franchises or other firms operating in the same specialist niche. What will make someone choose to talk to you over them?

Getting seen is the first battle.

There's an old joke among search engine optimisation (SEO) experts: "The best place to hide a dead body is the second page of Google search results." There's truth in it – the higher up the search rankings you appear for a given term, the more likely it is that someone will click through to your website. In fact, research shows that the top organic search result is ten times more likely to receive a click compared to one in tenth position.[1]

Getting found in search requires a combination of content marketing and SEO. Getting seen on social media also requires content and a knowledge of how to get your posts in front of the right people. How often you post, what you post, which hashtags you use and who you're connected with all matter. Finally, there's outbound marketing – getting yourself into the inboxes of existing clients and potential new ones and grabbing their attention.

Once you've made yourself known, the next struggle is converting that attention into business. Again, this is a combination of art and science. The science is in crafting a 'buyer journey', with a user experience (UX) that constantly nudges them towards a final commitment to make a purchase. The art is in creating copy and graphic design that sells your expertise and convinces them you are credible.

Another reason to take marketing seriously is the value it can add to your firm. We frequently work with clients who are thinking about their exit plan and want to maximise the sale price of their practice by building its client base and its brand.

Each year, global marketing agency Interbrand ranks the 100 most valuable brands in the world. It gives each brand on its list a financial value. Apple's brand, frequently at or near the top of the list, was valued at more than $320 billion in the most recent edition.[2]

Think about buying a house: you could buy a 'doer-upper' and add thousands to the value by extending the kitchen, converting the loft and installing double-glazing. Or you could take the easier path of purchasing a property somebody has already made look and feel smart and homely. By investing in your accountancy firm's brand and online presence, you're making it irresistible to future buyers and more appealing to potential clients.

---

[1] backlinko.com/google-ctr-stats   [2] interbrand.com/best-global-brands   **3**

Finally, there's the contribution marketing and branding make to business resilience. BrandZ is a brand equity database managed by the marketing firm Millward Brown. It is used to estimate the value of 100,000 individual business brands in 45 countries. Through customer surveys, the BrandZ researchers identify the strengths and weaknesses of each brand, identifying common traits among the fastest-growing businesses. It has been running since 2006 and that start date is important: it had benchmark figures for two years before the global financial crisis of 2008 and was therefore able to track the impact and aftermath of that cataclysmic event. A 2015 BrandZ report looked at the recovery of businesses in the wake of the 2008 financial crash and found that those with stronger brands recovered nine times faster than those without.[3]

Where do we start?

Here's the process we follow at a glance, from market research to measuring the success of your marketing strategy.

As with all processes, there has to be some flexibility in it. You might also find yourself going back to review previous stages as you progress. But, broadly speaking, this is it – a step-by-step, methodical approach. One bite-sized task after another. In the chapters that follow, we'll break all this down in detail, with practical exercises you can undertake.

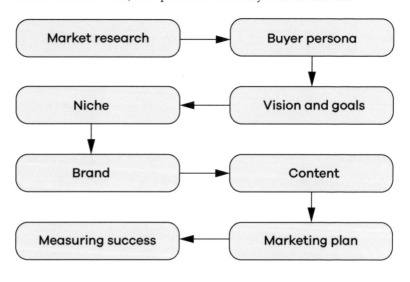

[3].brandz.com/report/global/2015

Chapter 2

Market research

In this chapter

You will learn:
Why market research is important. Understanding potential clients. The size and shape of the market. How to conduct your own research. *30 min read.*

For most accountancy firms, the first step will be market research. You need to know your enemy, know your clients and identify the opportunities you want to pursue.

In practice, very few of the firms we talk to have ever undertaken even basic market research. There are good reasons for this, not least that they often feel as if they've got an instinctive grasp of the regional or specialist markets in which they operate. Taking the time to check your assumption is always worthwhile, however – especially as (trust us) you'll often find they're wrong. In brief, here are the key steps:

1. Establish a hypothesis – what's the idea you want to test with your research? For example, "There is an untapped market for specialist advice for maritime businesses" or "We're undercharging for the level of service we provide".

2. Draw up a list of competitors and analyse their proposition, branding, website content and social media presence. Put simply, do they look better and more appealing than you?

3. Speak to existing clients. What do they like about the service you offer? What do they dislike? And what would they like to see more of?

4. Talk to non-clients in the sectors or segments you intend to target. What are their challenges? What do they need from an accountant? And why might they choose another firm over yours?

5. How big is the market you might be targeting? Do some desk research, looking at reports and stats from the Office for National Statistics, sector bodies and other reliable sources.

Speaking to your own clients can work well but in general, you'll get the most frank, useful feedback from those who don't know you and, to put it bluntly, don't care about your feelings. To find external research candidates, start by asking your colleagues and extended network if they know any in-target clients. Supplement that with call-outs on social media or by running a LinkedIn search and directly approaching people. Alternatively, you can commission an agency to find the right candidates on your behalf.

You may need to incentivise research participants. We recommend budgeting somewhere between £50 and £150 per candidate, although it really depends on the length of the interview and the candidates you're after. A high-net-worth individual isn't going to give up an hour of their valuable time for a few quid in Amazon vouchers.

In practice, getting people to attend interviews is hard, so make sure you have a list of reserve candidates in case some drop out. You should also allow plenty of time between interviews and relaying the results to allow for rescheduling or cancellations. Make sure you allow time between interviews (at least 30 minutes) and schedule them over a few days to allow yourself time to reflect and take stock. Before each interview, send an email and a meeting request setting out very clearly:

- the time
- date
- purpose of the conversation
- the medium – phone, video or in person?

When it comes to conducting interviews, aim to have one person asking questions and another taking notes. Alternatively, or additionally, record the interview, with the subject's permission. To avoid leading the candidate, ensure you create open-ended questions. Make them feel at ease but don't be afraid of silences – the less you talk, the more the candidate is likely to reveal. Try to ask each candidate the same questions, with the same wording, to make comparison easier. Sometimes, a candidate will ask a follow up question – "What do you mean by business advice?" If you can, try to turn the question back to them: "What do you think it means?"

After each meeting, the interviewer and note-taker should compare notes, fill in any gaps, correct any errors and collaborate on a quick summary of the headline findings.

Once all your interviews are complete, regroup to extract the key themes, significant quotes and stand-out details to form your conclusions. Resist the urge to shape the findings to match your own expectations or preferences – if the research tells you there's no demand for the service you had hoped to launch, it's best to accept it. Equally, if it reveals an exciting new avenue you hadn't considered, you'll want to explore that fully.

Most importantly, you should come away from this process with a clearer idea of your ideal client, ready to work up into buyer personas.

Market research checklist

- ☐ What's your hypothesis – what's the idea you are testing?
- ☐ Find candidates who will give you honest answers.
- ☐ Conduct interviews methodically.
- ☐ Reflect on the outputs to form your conclusion.

Chapter 3

Define your ideal client

Do you really know your ideal customer? Do you know where they get recommendations, what worries them and why they might buy from your competitor rather than from you? If not, it's time to create buyer personas.

Buyer personas are essentially imaginary individuals – avatars or proxies for whole groups of potential clients, often given typical names and typical faces. They're important because they provide a sharp, clear focus for your marketing strategy. They force you to direct your energy towards one, two or perhaps three specific, imaginary, perfect customers – to tailor your message and invest in the marketing activity that will generate the greatest return on investment.

The generally acknowledged inventor of the concept of buyer personas is Alan Cooper, a veteran software engineer. He told the story of his 1983 breakthrough himself in a 2008 blog post for his company, Cooper Professional Education:

> *"I was writing a critical-path project management programme that I called 'Plan*It.' Early in the project, I interviewed about seven or eight colleagues and acquaintances who were likely candidates to use a project management programme. In particular, I spoke at length with a woman named Kathy who worked at Carlick Advertising.*

> *"Kathy's job was called 'traffic' and it was her responsibility to assure that projects were staffed and staffers fully utilised. It seemed a classic project management task. Kathy was the basis for my first, primitive, persona."*[4]

Cooper undertook imaginary dialogues with 'Kathy', who acted as a stand-in for all the other project managers who might use the software he was engaged in designing:

> *"I found that this play-acting technique was remarkably effective for cutting through complex design questions of functionality and interaction, allowing me to clearly see what was necessary and unnecessary and, more importantly, to differentiate between what was used frequently and what was needed only infrequently."*

Essentially, the power of personas is this: it's easier to answer "What does Kathy want?" than it is to address the question "What do my customers want?"

Later, in the mid-1990s, working as a consultant, Cooper created three software user personas called Chuck, Cynthia and Rob. They didn't represent demographic segments based on gender, race, age or class but, rather, groups whose commonality was the goal they were trying to achieve and the obstacles they faced getting there. Cooper eventually set his idea out in a book called *The Inmates are Running the Asylum*, published in 1998, and before long, personas had gone viral in big business marketing circles.

Today, buyer personas (or customer personas as they're sometimes called) are often used to give marketing activity a clear target. To identify your perfect client or a key segment of your target audience, you need to gain an in-depth understanding of your customers:

- What are their challenges and the pain points in their lives?
- And what advice or information can make their lives easier?

---

[4] Now offline but formerly at cooper.com/journal/2008/05/the_origin_of_personas

A report we published in 2020, based on research with SMEs, revealed that 71% said it was important their accountant knew their industry sector.[5] The buyer persona is one way to go about crafting a marketing strategy that will show that understanding.

Those clients will see themselves and their needs reflected in your website copy, in the imagery you choose, the specific services you offer and the way you deliver them. They'll recognise their own stories in case studies and testimonials – proof that you really do have experience helping people like them.

Imagine an accountancy firm that focuses on the SME market, for example. They offer similar services to those provided by their competitors, and promote generic tax and business advice through their marketing, website messaging and blog content.

Then imagine a competing firm which has chosen to focus on, say, the construction industry. They've taken the time to understand the pain points and challenges faced by SMEs in that sector. They know what motivates those who own and operate companies in the field and what they want to achieve in their businesses. Accordingly, all their SME advice is tailored to those prospects. It answers their challenges and addresses their pain points. Every case study is from a building firm and every example they offer relates to construction. It's no longer generic SME advice – it's now vital information that speaks directly to those target clients.

If you compare those firms, which do you think the head of a house-building business is going to contact about their accounts?

The persona process

Knowing where to start when constructing personas can be a challenge. The easiest way into the process is to start by segmenting the clients you already have.

It might be that there are one or more clients who feel close to the ideal. Equally, there might be some who feel like a drain. Quickly turning them into rough buyer personas – name, age, sector – can be revealing. Discussing personas with accounting firms in brand strategy workshops we often hear variations of the same statement: "I think the problem is that we've got too many Mandys and not enough Fionas. We want more Fionas."

---

[5] 'What do SMEs want from accountants?', practiceweb.co.uk/knowledge/insight/

Once you've had this conversation, you should have the basis of your first persona ready to be worked up in more detail. At PracticeWeb, we start with a simple template.

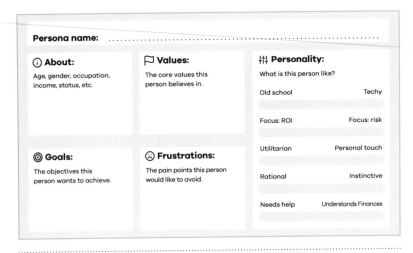

Fig 3.1. Blank Persona Template - download yours: https://bit.ly/3ALMCW7

Here's how that looks when it's been filled in:

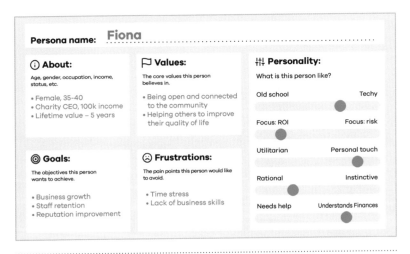

Fig 3.2. Finished Persona Template

The list of questions to ask yourself when developing personas can be virtually endless. The following five points should help get you started:

1. **Name** | This brings them to life and humanises your content.
2. **Occupation** | What is their role in the organisation?
3. **Age** | Are they just starting in business or looking towards exit?
4. **Gender** | This might or might not affect how you communicate.
5. **Income** | This influences the services they might buy.

That's a good start but the next five questions will provide further insight, helping you understand what makes them tick:

6. **Job details** | What are the ins and outs of their role? Are they hands-off decision makers or on the front line?
7. **Family** | This will influence their needs and, again, helps make the persona feel real.
8. **Career path** | Are they on the up, stagnating or struggling?
9. **Demeanour** | Are they businesslike or chatty? Stressed or relaxed? This will influence how you talk to and work with them.
10. **Communication** | Do they prefer phone calls, email or face-to-face contact?

Now that you have outlined a picture of the person it's time to think about the buyer journey:

- What are your target clients thinking at each stage of the buying journey?
- What are their challenges? (Their pain points.)
- What are they actually doing at each step?

Is there a major issue they're struggling with? Maybe their accounting software is out of date, they need more capital to expand, or require guidance around staffing options.

An example of a pain point for the buyer journey shown below is "I need help with staying on top of the money coming in and out of the business." That suggests they might benefit from bookkeeping services.

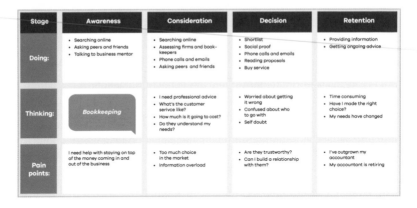

Stage	Awareness	Consideration	Decision	Retention
Doing:	• Searching online • Asking peers and friends • Talking to business mentor	• Searching online • Assessing firms and book-keepers • Phone calls and emails • Asking peers and friends	• Shortlist • Social proof • Phone calls and emails • Reading proposals • Buy service	• Providing information • Getting ongoing advice
Thinking:	*Bookkeeping*	• I need professional advice • What's the customer serivce like? • How much is it going to cost? • Do they understand my needs?	• Worried about getting it wrong • Confused about who to go with • Self doubt	• Time consuming • Have I made the right choice? • My needs have changed
Pain points:	I need help with staying on top of the money coming in and out of the business	• Too much choice in the market • Information overload	• Are they trustworthy? • Can I build a relationship with them?	• I've outgrown my accountant • My accountant is retiring

Fig 3.3. Example buyer journey template. Get yours: https://bit.ly/3ALMCW7

You'll see that the journey breaks down into four stages:
- awareness – research
- consideration – reflecting
- decision – crunch time
- retention – after they've signed up

Think about the questions someone who might need help with bookkeeping will be asking about your offer at each of those four stages, and the anxieties they might have. Your content needs to pre-emptively answer those concerns, demonstrate empathy and prove that you understand their challenges. When we talk about building an emotional connection, this is what we mean – not signing off your emails with three kisses.

An emotional connection with a business startup owner who is looking for their first accountant will be quite different to that with a multi-million-pound business tycoon nearing retirement. Present content which connects with your audience, explains the benefits of your service and shows how you can really, practically help them.

While working up the persona for Fiona, it's likely that you caught yourself thinking about aspects of your ideal client that don't quite fit. Resist the temptation to make your first persona too general. Instead, use those notes as the basis of your second persona, or even a third.

Your buyer personas might all be in the same sector but at different stages in their career, or with different sized businesses. Or they could be vastly different.

Workshopping personas with one PracticeWeb client, we came up with three personas:

- Vipul, a pharmacist
- Dimitrius, a restaurant entrepreneur
- Raj, a convenience store owner

They have some things in common – geographical location, a focus on the high street – but differ in some important ways. Giving each its own persona allows for flexibility while remaining focused.

Buyer persona checklist

- [ ] Develop personas which match your ideal clients.
- [ ] Start with name, job title and basic demographics.
- [ ] Add more depth and detail.
- [ ] Reflect on the buyer journey including pain points.

Chapter 4

Set your vision and goals

In this chapter

You will learn:
The difference between vision and goals. Mapping business goals to marketing. Communicating vision and goals to your team. *30 min read.*

▶ **Exercise** Identify your business goals. *30 mins*

What do you want to achieve? That's the big question that should drive your marketing strategy. Here are a couple of examples based on the vision statements of accountancy firms PracticeWeb has worked with in recent years:

- Increase market share by becoming the go-to accountancy brand for residential property landlords.
- Achieve a 5% growth in client base with profitable clients we actually like – trust and chemistry.
- Increase turnover to half a million per year by attracting clients who want to contribute to society, do things properly and pay a fair amount of tax.

The foundation of any leadership strategy is setting direction. You need to show people in the company that it's part of something bigger and create a feeling of organisational self-worth. For accounting firms, that means creating a sense of something beyond the bread-and-butter business of crunching numbers. How does your work help people, families, communities and industry sectors thrive and survive?

Setting a big target with a three to five year deadline, and clarity on what success will look like, is the best way to motivate your teams and keep your marketing strategy on track.

Setting goals

The building blocks of a vision are goals – the specific, concrete items around turnover and growth you can see in the examples above. Other examples we've encountered over the years include:

- Pay off my mortgage by the age of 35. (A solo accountant.)
- Be back at 2019 turnover by mid-2021.
- Get more SME clients and reduce reliance on contractors.
- Get 50 new clients per month.
- Increase value of firm by 25% prior to exit.

Once you've established business goals, it's time to think about marketing goals. Again, marketing should always serve the business and never be undertaken for its own sake. Here's an example of business goals mapped against marketing.

Business goals	Marketing goals
Generate £X new revenue by year-end	• Generate £X new sales leads over the year
Target new customer segment	• Build brand awareness • Educate buyers • Establish expertise • A nurture programme for leads
Launch new service	• Educate buyers • Generate £X new sales leads over the year • Build awareness of service • Identify cross-sell/upsell opportunities • A nurture programme for leads

The last step in the process of setting vision and goals is communicating all of this to your team. Some or all of them may have been involved in the workshopping process – that's often how you get the best results – but you need everyone in the firm to know and understand the direction of travel.

First, make sure you're confident in telling the story. Set it out in a presentation, following the hierarchy set out above: vision, business goals and marketing goals. Make sure that the logic is clear and try to anticipate any challenges you might get from team members.

The trick to really embedding the vision and goals is providing it in multiple formats and repeating it. A typical approach might be an all-staff presentation followed by an email attaching the slides and summarising the key points. You might then find it useful to include a vision statement at the start of staff meetings and in any update emails you send out, at least for the first few months. It's not uncommon to see a version of the vision up on the wall of the office and that can be really helpful in driving it home.

The absolutely most important thing you have to do, though, is demonstrate your commitment to the vision in your decisions and actions – and signpost the connection when the opportunity arises. For example, "We're launching a new R&D tax relief service because of our commitment to getting more tech startup clients by 2023."

Identify your business goals

Time: 30 minutes

1. First, with your team or on your own, get a pen and paper, or some sticky notes, and write down as many possible goals as you can in five minutes. Be ambitious and don't self-censor – there's no such thing as a silly idea at this stage. Think about the ideal client (your buyer personas) and ask yourself:

   - What does the firm look like in three years' time? What awards might you have won? Which new services will you have launched? Which dream clients will you have acquired?
   - What are you dissatisfied with at present? What needs to change?
   - As an owner or partner, what are your personal goals?

2. Next, get everyone's ideas together and sort them, grouping similar suggestions. Then ask everyone to pick their top three by marking them with a dot. (You can do this on your own, too, but it's not as much fun.)

3. Take the five or six with the most votes and, on a clean sheet, set those out. Then discuss and refine each potential goal, making sure to add dates and numbers where possible – they need to be specific and quantifiable.

Vision and goals checklist

- ☐ Reflect on market research and personas
- ☐ Define a long-term vision
- ☐ Break that down into specific business goals
- ☐ Map business goals against marketing
- ☐ Communicate vision and goals to your team

Chapter 5

Find a niche

In this chapter

You will learn:
Different ways to find a niche.
Shaping your proposition.
30 min read.

▶ **Exercise 1** Identify your niche.
30 mins

▶ **Exercise 2** Write your value
positioning statement. *30 mins*

We always advise accountancy firms to consider finding a niche.
Why? Because it's the simplest way to stand out in a crowded market
and to focus your marketing activity.

You'll notice that PracticeWeb, for example, only works with
accountants. That's a great example of nicheing – and it's served us
well for more than 20 years. Among our clients, we have accountancy
firms which specialise in working with landlords, retailers, creative
businesses, charities and with super-wealthy individuals living overseas.
Some target older clients considering retirement while others are after
twenty-something startup owners.

From that list, you should pick up a key point: finding a niche doesn't
necessarily have to mean focusing on a single industry sector. Instead, we
suggest considering a wide range of possible points of difference.

Price

Does your point of difference need to reflect a certain price
point? Is it luxury, discount or moderate? Don't read value judge-
ments into those – there's nothing wrong with either exclusivity
or good value. It's just a case of knowing where you are and being
the best you can within that bracket.

Demographics

This is if you consider things like age, gender or income level to be part of the proposition. Consider your ideal clients and if they have certain commonalities in their demographics that mean you should reflect this in your point of difference.

Quality

If you consider the quality of service you provide as a key differentiator for your firm, think about if it's premium, tailored, or economical. Again, it's fine to be any of those as it's a case of acknowledging where you are and meeting your clients' expectations.

Psychographics

This is about your ideal clients' interests, values or attitudes. Perhaps your practice works with charities or ethical businesses. This may be a key differentiator and a clear niche focus.

Sector

This is about the sectors you serve. This could be multiple sectors, or a single sector. If you want sectors to form part of your position, consider any commonalities. If you want to be sector-agnostic, you may want to consider referencing that also in your proposition.

The key to defining your niche is understanding what your ideal clients value. If you've defined one or more buyer personas as set out in the last chapter, you'll have a head start, and a niche may well suggest itself. For example, 'High street businesses' covers the pharmacist, restaurateur and convenience store owner identified as key personas by one of our clients.

It's worth saying, too, that there are certain supposed points of difference which... aren't. These are ideas that many firms are already using and that, to potential clients, barely register as anything more than background noise. They're cliches, in other words.

'Friendly and professional'

This is one of the most common terms we see used by accountancy firms. Would any prospect expect you to be anything other than professional or friendly? It can be a good place to start but we'd always advise pushing on to find something more interesting.

'Not your typical accountant'

Just run a quick Google search to see how many practices are using this phrase or similar. It's common and not a strong point of difference. If you position yourself this way at present, think about how you demonstrate your difference rather than just declaring.

'Big enough to cope, small enough to care'

Like 'professional and friendly', this is hedging, not differentiating. A long-winded way of saying you're medium-sized. Again, you can use copy, imagery and content to make this point in a more interesting way.

As well as cliches, there are some key mistakes to avoid.

You can't appeal to everyone

You'll end up coming across as generic and risk appealing to nobody in particular.

Aim high

Aspirational leadership is contagious. Build something your teams can get behind, that your clients can buy into and that will appeal to your prospects.

Be honest

If you make false claims, or say things that don't believe in your heart of hearts, clients, prospects and your team will see through it and trust will be damaged.

Don't copy others

As tempting as it might be to emulate someone who's successful or who you admire, it isn't the way to build a strong brand. Draw inspiration from them, sure, but let that be the starting point for your own journey.

In our brand strategy workshop, we use a framework to help accounting firms define their unique brand and proposition. It's anchored around three key questions:

- What are you deeply passionate about?
- What are you really good at?
- What drives your economic engine?

Whatever sits at the centre of the Venn diagram should be the basis of your proposition – an elevator pitch, if you like.

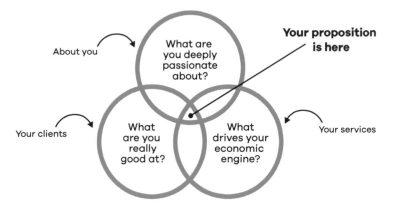

Let's say your team is really good at processing tax returns quickly and accurately; you particularly enjoy working with builders and tradespeople; and, as it happens, you've got quite a lot of them on your books already. That suggests that you could and probably should lean into that:

We produce fast, accurate tax returns for construction industry specialists, including CIS refunds, starting at £150.

Find a niche

Time: 30 minutes

1. On your own, with your fellow partners or with a project team, spend five minutes writing down answers to the following questions:

   - **What do your buyer personas all have in common?**
     Eg they're all SMEs in West Cornwall; they're all focused on growth; they're all online businesses.
   - **What is your firm deeply passionate about?**
     Eg working with tech startups; social enterprises; helping older people retain their hard-earned wealth.
   - **What are you really good at?**
     Eg fast, efficient tax returns; R&D tax relief claims; tax planning for non-residents.
   - **What drives your economic engine?**
     Eg multi-property landlords with complex tax needs; growth planning for larger SME manu-facturing businesses.

2. Get everyone's ideas together and sort them, grouping similar suggestions across all three cate-gories. Discard anything suggested only once.

3. Take the two or three with the most votes and, on a clean sheet, set those out. Then discuss and refine, combining suggestions if appropriate.

4. Choose one and write it out as a clear, simple description of a possible niche.

Write your value positioning statement

Time: 30 minutes

On your own or with colleagues, fill in the blanks in this template:

For [target customers] who need to [statement of need], our [product or service] provides [unique benefits].

You might put it up on a whiteboard and use sticky notes to brainstorm ideas, or do something similar in a virtual setting with Miro or a Google Jamboard.

Start by getting lots of ideas up on the board, then pick your favourites, then refine them in a second, third and fourth pass.

Keep reading it out loud as you go – when it's right, everyone in the room will know.

Here's an example of a finished statement:

For **gardeners and landscapers without dedicated office space** who need to **process staff payroll,** our **outsourced service** provides **easy access to reports through a smartphone app.**

Niche checklist

- ☐ Review market research, personas and vision
- ☐ Run a niche identification exercise
- ☐ Define a simple, clear statement of your niche
- ☐ Define your proposition and produce an elevator pitch

Chapter 6

Forge a brand

In this chapter

You will learn:
Brand vs branding vs brand identity. Brand values and promises. Brand identity and assets: logo, colour palette, typography. Tone of voice. *30 min read.*

▶ **Exercise 1.** What are your brand values. *45 mins*

▶ **Exercise 2.** Who are you? *30 mins*

As well as the services you offer and the niche you target, your brand can also go a long way to setting you apart from the competition. Before we get into how, let's get the terminology straight.

When it comes to creating a brand, businesses usually think about designing a logo; choosing the brand colours; fonts; and other assets that require design input, such as business cards and websites. This is actually the end part of the process, rather than the beginning.

To create a strong brand we need to understand three distinct terms – brand, branding and brand identity.

Brand is the meaning that people attach to your firm. Amazon magnate Jeff Bezos says "your brand is what other people say about you when you're not in the room". In other words, brand is everything we know, think and feel about a company. It is its meaning and the story that goes along with its name.

Branding is about how you convey that meaning in everything you do. How do you want to come across? Loud, exciting and youthful? Or calm, thoughtful and mature? Branding is what your customers experience each time they interact with your firm and influences the way they think about it.

Brand identity is the practical nuts-and-bolts end of branding – the elements used to identify a brand. Fonts, colours, logo, photography style – all of these are the assets you use to help the audience recognise you, remember you and distinguish you from the competition. A strong brand identity is distinctive and painstakingly consistent. Here's a test: if a client saw a billboard without your firm's name on it but using your palette, typography and a slogan in your tone of voice, would they know it was yours?

There are big advantages to building a strong brand. First, it enables you to sell on value, not just on price. Your clients are buying into your values and the qualities they consider you to possess, just as some identify at a deep level as Apple users while others wear Linux hoodies. You'll be appealing directly to your ideal clients, demonstrating you understand them and their needs, and thus making yourself the clear choice over the competition.

The follow on from that is loyalty. If people buy into your brand, as long as you keep delivering on promises and living up to expectations, you'll be rewarded with better customer retention and clients who are happy to refer your services to others.

There's a final benefit to being unique: the impossibility of true comparison. If a client can see several firms with similar cultures, selling similar services at similar prices, they might start asking why you are more expensive, or why you don't offer X, Y or Z as part of your package. A truly distinctive brand makes answering that easy: 'You could go with them, but they're not us, are they?'

Brand values, purpose and promises

If you've been reading through the previous chapters one after the other, you may have noticed some overlap between the ideas that come up at each stage in the digital marketing process. You might well be thinking that the concept of brand values sounds an awful lot like the vision we talked about in chapter 4 and, yes, they're certainly part of the same conversation. When we run brand strategy workshops with PracticeWeb clients, we start by talking about vision and goals and move on to define brand values, brand purpose and brand promises – there's a continuity there.

Brand values should complete the statement "Our firm believes in…" or, more obviously, "We value…" They're useful as a tool for making sure everyone in the business is pulling in the same direction and as a test for everything you do. Let's look at some examples. First, here are the brand values that underpin all of Coca-Cola's marketing. Coca-Cola believes in…

- Leadership – the courage to shape a better future
- Collaboration – leverage collective genius
- Integrity – be real
- Accountability – if it is to be, it's up to me
- Passion – committed in heart and mind
- Diversity – as inclusive as our brands
- Quality – what we do, we do well

If you were a manager at Coke, you'd no doubt be expected to explain how any proposal or project meets those values. Does it demonstrate leadership? Does it reflect diversity? And so on. Closer to home, these are the values for cloud accounting software provider Xero:

- human
- ownership
- champion
- challenge
- beautiful

You'll note those don't quite follow the simple rule we've established above – you can't use them to complete a sentence. If they'd come to us for help with their marketing, we'd probably have tidied them up and rewritten them. But hopefully you get the point – and you can certainly see 'beautiful' and 'human' shining through in much of Xero's work, even as it's grown to become an international brand.

Finally here's a set of brand values for an accountancy firm based on those that emerged from a client workshop we ran in 2019. *See over.*

This firm believes in...

Community	Empathy
We care about the impact we have on our people, our clients, their family and North Yorkshire.	We always take the time to put ourselves in our clients' shoes – what do they really need from us right now?
The future	**Progress**
From farmers to sole traders, everyone deserves to benefit from the power of technology.	We're always a step ahead of the competition and aim to be better than we were yesterday.

Brand purpose is a clear, simple statement of your firm's **why, how and what.** Why does your firm exist? To give rural businesses in North Yorkshire the same fighting chance as those in cities or down south. How does it do it? By fighting stereotypes about agricultural businesses and offering services on the basis that they're as hungry and forward-looking as anyone else. What form does that support take? Cloud accounting setup and training with busy farmers in mind.

The next step in our brand process is to establish **brand promises.** These are another complementary tool designed to help you think about and express what your values mean for your clients in practice. They should complete the sentences "We will always..." or, more literally, "We promise to..." Here are the brand promises that accompany the brand values in the example above.

- Contribute to rural communities in North Yorkshire.
- Take time to listen and provide what's needed most.
- Recognise that our clients are tech-savvy and forward-looking.
- Improve our knowledge, processes and standards every day.

The truth is, the process of defining your values, purpose and promises is almost as important as the finished product. The discussion you have will shake out and hopefully resolve disagreements between partners. It will allow your team members to talk positively, with excitement, about what motivates them. And it will push you to focus on your clients and how you can be different to, and better than, the competition.

Brand identity and assets

Finally, here it is – the exciting creative stuff we all enjoy but which should be the end point of your branding journey, never the start. Designers and copywriters thrive on input from the client. The process you'll have been through to arrive at vision, goals, brand values and so on, means that you're able to provide them with a comprehensive readout of the messages you want your brand identity to communicate.

In an ideal world, your **logo** should be the ultimate distillation of what your firm is about – everything boiled down to a single, instantly recognisable mark. And one that you'll potentially be living with for years. The best logos have a lot of depth and convey a complex message full of meaning, while at the same time looking clean and simple. That's why professional marketers shudder with horror at the idea of quick, cheap logos, which are generally disastrous.

Here are some examples of logos PracticeWeb's designers have produced in the past few years:

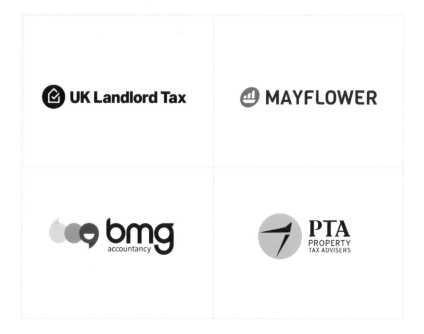

In each case, the apparent simplicity is the result of a lot of hard work and thought beforehand. Consider the Mayflower Accounting logo in particular. That elegant, minimal mark represents both a ship (exploration) and a bar graph demonstrating growth, which reflects the brand vision and values. And here are just some of the iterations it went through before that final version came together:

If in doubt, or if your budget is limited, keep your logo simple in the first instance. It's better just to have the name of the firm in clear, legible type than lots of badly-conceived graphics and flourishes.

When it comes to **colour palettes**, accountants have a reputation for conservatism and, in particular, for clinging to a safe, rather muted shade of blue. Blue isn't in itself bad – it's often used to signify trust, intelligence and stability. But look at any breakout accountancy brand – dare we mention Crunch? – and you'll note that they immediately stand out with a distinctly different palette.

Designers draw upon a whole body of research and best practice known as colour theory. It ascribes values, ideas and temperament to colours and shades. Bright red, for example, is regarded as 'hot' and associated with fire, war and violence. There's a reason so many poisonous creatures in nature have evolved red colouring. But it's also the colour of love, passion and excitement – the ultimate accent if you need to draw someone's attention. Colour theory also guides how colours are combined to create palettes with primary, secondary and accent colours.

One final important aspect of brand design is **typography** or, in layman's terms, fonts. The font you use can say a lot about your accountancy firm's brand and personality but with so many available, choosing can be difficult.

There are two main categories of font – serif and sans-serif. The most famous example of a serif font, simply because it's installed on almost every computer in the world, is Times New Roman. Serif fonts are based on classical forms – the kind of lettering you might see carved into stone in ancient Rome – and the early days of the printing press. That's why they suggest conservatism, seriousness and tradition. Think *The Times* or *Daily Telegraph*. When we're dealing with a firm that wants to convey traditionalism, quality and thoughtfulness, we'll often look at serif fonts first.

Sans-serif fonts emerged in the 19th century but really became popular in the 20th. With their clean lines they chimed with modernist design from Art Deco to minimalism, and in the 21st century are popular with tech companies such as Apple and Google. The most famous sans-serif font is undoubtedly Helvetica – it even has its own documentary film. Rail Alphabet, the font traditionally used on the British train network, is another example. Geometric sans-serif fonts such as Futura are subtly different – they might render the letter O as a perfect circle, for example – and there are also what are known as humanist sans-serif fonts, such as Gill Sans. Sans-serif fonts can suit accountants that identify as modern, open and bright.

In many cases, the typographic guidance we devise for accountancy firms will combine serif and sans-serif fonts for contrast, balance and legibility.

Tone of voice

Along with design, how your firm expresses itself in writing is another important aspect of brand. There's more on this in chapter 8, 'The power of content', but for now, let's focus on copywriting, which goes hand in hand with graphic design. As with visuals, your brand tone of voice needs to flow from your vision and values. Is your firm conservative and discreet? Progressive and energetic? Modern and informal? Those things will need to be reflected in everything from vocabulary to punctuation.

There are some shortcuts for thinking about tone of voice which, after all, can feel quite abstract. One of the strategies we use in content workshops and consultations is to ask some simple questions:

- If your firm had a TV ad, who would do the voiceover?
- If you were a car brand, which would it be?
- Is your tone more like *The Sun* or *The Times*?

The first question prompts all kinds of interesting responses, including Russell Brand, James Earl Jones (the voice of Darth Vader), Vicky McClure from Line of Duty, Sean Bean, Olivia Colman, Ray Winstone and (surprisingly often) Stephen Fry. When we ask "Why?" even more useful ideas emerge. Take Stephen Fry, for example – he's regarded as clever but likeable, charming, reassuring and approachable. Vicky McClure was chosen because she was local (she has a Nottingham accent), strong, direct and sharp. That all feeds into our copywriting process.

More literally, when you're writing headings and slogans, it can be helpful to hear them in the voice of the chosen avatar: "No, I don't think Sean Bean would say that." Sometimes, there's no need to reach for an external tone of voice. If your firm has founders, owners or partners with strong voices of their own, that can be enough. It's just a matter of making sure third-party copywriters get to spend time with those individuals, soaking up their mannerisms and voices. Either way, it needs to be codified as rules or guidance, such as:

- use relatively short sentences
- employ contractions freely
- colloquialisms are OK, but aim for northern – never cockney
- use positive, cheerful language
- ask lots of questions in the copy.

Who are you?

Time: 30 minutes

First, on your own or in a group, answer the following questions:

1. If your firm had a TV ad, who would do the voiceover?

2. Which car brand is closest to your firm?

3. Which supermarket?

4. And which newspaper or magazine?

Then go through the list and discuss why each name or brand is there – what is it about them that seems similar to your firm? For example, BMW cars are well-engineered but understated; the *Economist* is intellectual and focused on detail; Sainsbury's is warm and sensibly priced.

Finally, use that second list to write out a description that could apply to your firm's tone of voice, eg "We are warm, enthusiastic and good humoured."

Brand checklist

The point of all the above is that to construct a robust, enduring brand, you can't do anything casually, quickly or on the cheap. Every image, colour and word should be thought about and carefully chosen to support the underlying vision and values.

- [ ] Clear, distinctive proposition (elevator pitch)
- [ ] Unique brand – what do people say about your firm?
- [ ] Authenticity – do you and your team believe in it?
- [ ] Brand identity
    - [ ] logo
    - [ ] typography
    - [ ] colour palette
    - [ ] tone of voice

Chapter 7

Get the perfect website

In this chapter

You will learn:
Do you need a website? Is your
current website good enough?
How to structure your website for
maximum effect.
20 min read.

▶ **Exercise** Quick and easy user
testing. *45 mins*

**For most accountants the cornerstone of your online presence will
be your website.** It's a shopfront, lead generation machine and content hub all in one. In this chapter, we're going to explain how you can
assess the health and quality of your current website, and set out some
best practice for accountancy firm websites.

First, though, as always, let's pin down the terminology: a website is a set of interconnected web pages, usually with a distinct name
(eg YouTube) and domain name (eg youtube.com), stored on a web
server and made available on the internet. There are lots of ways to
have a presence online – a business page on Facebook, for example, or
a Twitter profile, or a free page via wordpress.com or Wix – but that's
not the same as having a website. Only with your own website, and
your own domain, do you have the power to completely control the
user experience and shape the buyer journey.

Do you need a website? Yes, definitely, if you have any intention
of acquiring new clients. It's possible that yours is one of the handful
of accountancy practices that gets sufficient business through word
of mouth, networking and passing trade on the high street. Especially
if yours is a small firm just starting out, you might find that a strong

social media presence is doing the job. If you've got any ambition, though, building a website is the first step – and these days, prospective clients will probably look for a modern, good quality website as a sign of your credibility. There's a sense that a business that doesn't have a website doesn't really exist.

But do you need an up-to-date website? If your current website is more than, say, two years old, it's certainly going to be worth giving it an MOT. Technology and client expectations change quickly in the digital world. For example, hardly anyone was browsing on mobile devices like phones or tablets a decade ago. Now, more than 60% of Google searches are from mobile devices, and Google actually uses the mobile version of your site to assess quality rather than the version presented to desktop PCs.

Some other signs that your website might be out of date or underperforming include:

- **Invisible** – there could be technical faults causing Google to penalise your website in the rankings, even if you have plenty of decent quality content.
- **HTTP, not HTTPS** – if your website address begins with HTTP rather than HTTPS, not only will users feel less confident in the safety of your site but you might also find that Google ranks it lower. The S in HTTPS stands for 'secure' and HTTPS is effectively a seal of approval guaranteeing the safety of the connection between a user's browser and the website in question.
- **Slow loading** – websites that are slow to load tend to rank lower in Google search results, quite apart from the fact that they're off-putting to potential clients.
- **Confusing** – potential clients who land on your website need to be able to find the information they need quickly and easily.
- **Doesn't reflect your brand** – if the design and content of your website doesn't speak to your ideal clients, they'll click away.

Simple user testing for your website

Time: 45 minutes

It can be hard to be objective about your own website because you'll have got used to it, know its quirks and probably helped design it. That's why this exercise can be so eye-opening.

First, identify two or three people who aren't involved with your practice on a regular basis and don't know your website well. If they're not especially tech savvy, all the better.

Then sit them down at a PC, or with a mobile device, and ask them to complete the following simple tasks while you observe – silently!

1. Find the homepage of the firm's website by searching Google.

2. Starting on the homepage, find the firm's telephone number.

3. Identify one sector or group with which the firm specialises in working.

4. Find the blog and navigate to a blog post relating to that sector specialism.

5. Find a contact form and send a message with the subject line TEST.

Resist the temptation to offer advice or answer any questions they ask; just say "What do you think you need to do?" or similar.

If there are problems, you'll hopefully have seen them for yourself, but, finally, ask them to rate their experience out of five, where five is good and one is bad.

- How easy was the site to find?
- Was it easy to use?
- Was it fast (five) or slow (one)?
- How likely would you be to use the firm based on the website?

Website architecture and structure

Function should dictate form, not the other way round.

Architecture refers to how the information on your website is structured, including hierarchy and connections between items of information. It's fairly abstract and technical but overlaps with the more practical business of website structure. **Structure** refers to concrete questions of which pages you have on your website, how they're organised and interlinked, and how they're displayed in the navigation. When we're building websites for clients, this is often where we start, compiling a list of the information we have and want to convey, and then sketching out a structure.

As a rule, avoid coming up with a clever-clever structure for the sake of being different. Certain conventions have arisen purely because they work for users and provide familiar reference points to help them on their journey. For example, eCommerce websites often have a big search box at the top and centre of the screen, because user testing over the years has shown that people expect it to be there. In the case of accountancy firm websites, though there aren't quite the same well-rehearsed expectations, certain elements of good practice have emerged.

Think of the dream client visiting your site for the first time – what do they want to find?

First, they might want proof that you offer the specific account-ancy service they're looking to acquire. In which case, it's important to have information about your offer on your homepage.

Then, assuming they want to know more, they need to be able to find a more detailed note on exactly what your service includes without hunting around. In practice, that probably means an element in the navigation bar that says 'Our services', or some close synonym, linking through to individual service pages.

If you work across multiple industry sectors, a 'Sectors' menu is also a good idea, directing prospects to individual pages demonstrat-ing that you really do know their industry and explaining how you tailor your service to its particular requirements.

Or let's say they want more general proof of your expertise and experience – what will they be looking for? Partner profiles on a 'Meet the team' page under 'About us', perhaps, telling a compelling story about how your team developed its unique mix of skills.

Maybe they want to know about your firm's culture – do you share their attitudes? Are you the kind of people with whom they can do business? This is where 'How we work' or 'Our approach' comes in, setting out a philosophy and approach.

And if they just want to get in touch, there has to be an obvious place to 'Contact us'.

That's just a snapshot of some of the key sections your website might need. Depending on your firm's specialisms, you might need more pages, or fewer.

Another general rule: in terms of search engine performance, the more pages the better, within reason. The more text you provide, the more there is for Google to get to grips with, and the more likely it is that you'll meet the needs of users who have come to your website looking for information or answers.

Website checklist

- ☐ Review marketing goals
- ☐ What is the purpose of your website?
- ☐ Audit your current website with user testing
- ☐ Test that your site is user friendly
- ☐ Check for spelling and grammatical errors
- ☐ Review how fast your website loads
- ☐ Make sure you have clear calls to action
- ☐ Secure your website through HTTPS
- ☐ Set up Google analytics to track performance
- ☐ Create landing pages for key services and sectors
- ☐ Assess your website's mobile-friendliness
- ☐ Add your professional body logo to your site
- ☐ Make sure you have a contact page

Chapter 8

The power of content

In this chapter

You will learn:
What is content marketing?
Defining content marketing goals.
Different types of content: copy,
blog posts, social media. Content
planning. *20 min read.*

▶ **Exercise 1** Define your content goals. *30 mins*

▶ **Exercise 2** Build a six-month
content calendar. *30 mins*

Content marketing is the process of generating interest in and engagement with your firm by providing material that will be genuinely helpful for clients and prospective clients.

Content marketing isn't a new thing. In the *Mad Men* era, big companies used to produce calendars, almanacks, guidebooks, magazines and all sorts of similar collateral. *The Guinness Book of Records* and the *Michelin Guide* are two famous examples of content marketing, putting the names of a brewery and tyre manufacturer respectively into homes all around the world. In that respect, content marketing shares some similarities with 'advertorial', which presents advertising copy as if it is a feature article or television programme.

With the coming of the internet, though, content marketing really came into its own. Securing business in the 21st century depends in large part on getting people to visit your website which means two things:

1. **Giving them something to engage with** – content they'll want to read, watch and hopefully share.
2. **Making sure it surfaces in web searches** – providing keyword-rich, substantial, authoritative copy that Google can get its teeth into.

The good news is that these are mutually compatible goals. On the whole, content that works for readers also works for Google, which is designed to surface material which its algorithms judge to exhibit expertise, authority and trust (EAT).

Accountants have a distinct advantage in that they are by definition expert, authoritative and trusted, thanks to the system of qualifications and institutional checks and balances within which they operate. We also know that tax and finance are subjects on which people are particularly hungry for clear, consistent information. One of our clients, for example, derives around 78% of total traffic to their website – thousands of visits a month – from a single informative blog post on inheritance tax.

But of course there's bad news, too: there are no shortcuts or dodges. Producing interesting, credible content requires time, effort and thought. A decade or so ago, when Google's algorithm was much less sophisticated, it was possible to game the system with trash content stuffed with keywords. This kind of thing would rank highly and win raw clicks but it infuriated and frustrated users. Google penalises it, users won't engage with it, and it damages the credibility of brands that do it.

That's not to say that creating or commissioning quality content has to be a nightmare. There are certain processes you can follow, and good practice to which you can adhere, that can make it, if not easy, then at least painless.

Define content marketing goals

Don't dive straight into creating content – pause, take a breath, and think. Content should be the end point of the process, not the beginning. If you're producing content for the sake of it, without a specific aim in mind, it will read as fluff and alienate those whose attention you're seeking to grab. So, what do you want your content to achieve? Some common goals for accountancy firms include:

- Generating leads among specific target client groups, eg farmers, or creative agencies.
- Raising the profile of a specific service or aspect of your firm's business, eg cloud accounting.

- Setting out what differentiates your firm from the competition, eg fixed fees, or advisory services.
- Improving search rankings by answering demand for specific information revealed through keyword analysis. For example, is there an untapped desire for information on R&D tax credits in your town or region?

A sensible approach is, first, to determine two or three overarching goals that apply to your body of content in its entirety, ideally prioritised. Working out what you want to achieve will immediately give shape to your communications: if what you're doing doesn't contribute to those objectives, why are you doing it? Conversely, you might find that it helps identify where investment of time and effort is most valuable because a single piece of work will hit more than one marketing target. In our content strategy workshops, we ask people to answer the following questions to help define content objectives:

1. How can our content attract new customers?
2. How can our content help existing customers?
3. What can our content reveal about us?
4. What should our content make people think?
5. How should our content make people feel?
6. What should our content make people do?

In chapter 3, we talked about defining the ideal client through buyer personas. This is one exercise where those are especially useful. With Fiona the charity CEO in mind, how might you answer the above questions?

- **Attract** by ranking highly in search results for key questions around charity accounting.
- **Reveal** that we've got a partner dedicated to charity accounting, who sits on the boards of several charities.
- **Think** that we really know the charities SORP inside out.
- **Feel** that the team really cares and is committed to the sector.
- **Act** by getting in touch for an initial consultation.

That tells us immediately that we're going to need content that demonstrates expertise, goes into specific detail and conveys the values of the firm.

Exercise 1

Define your content objectives

Time: 30 minutes

On your own or in a group, spend ten minutes writing down on sticky notes as many answers as possible to the following questions:

- How can our content attract new customers?
- How can our content help existing customers?
- What can our content reveal about us?
- What should our content make people think?
- How should our content make people feel?
- What should our content make people do?

Number them so you'll know which questions were being answered – though it doesn't matter too much if they get mixed up.

Then get everyone's sticky notes together and group those which are the same or similar. You might start to see some obvious candidates at this point. If not (a) discard any that only came up once and (b) ask people to vote on the others, aiming for three or four final objectives.

Then rewrite them on a clean sheet so that each one completes the sentence "Our content should...", eg "Our content should help us rank for keywords around VAT".

Types of content

In our experience, when we talk about content, most people immediately think of blog posts. That's because typically the blog is the section of the website that users expect to have a flow of new content and which, if neglected, most quickly gets out of date. (There's not much sadder than the sight of a company blog last updated in 2016.) In reality, however, content takes many forms, such as:

- website pages
- social media feeds
- press releases
- eBooks
- research reports
- email newsletters
- video.

Different types of content ought to be weighted differently. **Website** copy, for example, has a long shelf life and ought to be crafted and polished to the Nth degree. Every word should be chosen with care, every punctuation mark purposefully selected and, ideally, house style and tone of voice documented for future reference. **Blog posts**, on the other hand, can afford to be a little less polished – a steady flow of content and topicality are arguably more important than absolute perfection. **Social media posts** are the most transitory of all – the average life of a Tweet is reckoned to be something like eight minutes – and so even more than with blog posts, focus on a constant supply of material rather than spending hours constructing the perfect 280 characters. To employ a rather ripe analogy, it's a bit like the difference between restaurant meals, weekday dinners, and on-the-move snacks.

With website copy in mind, it's worth taking a moment to reflect on website structure and the relative value of different content types in terms of SEO. Accountancy service and sector-specific pages, though they might seem rather dull to put together, are hugely beneficial in terms of attracting prospects via web searches. That's because people typically look for something quite specific and so a permanent page which mentions that specific topic is typically most likely to turn up in results.

This content is rarely inspiring but that doesn't mean it's not useful or relevant, or that it can't help to communicate your brand. It is really good at removing ambiguity – at saying, clearly and straightforwardly, that, yes, you do provide that particular service, for that specific type of client. It takes a step out of the buyer journey and moves a potential client closer to the point where they decide to work with you.

In terms of search engine rankings, pages are also generally more valuable for SEO than blog posts, and blog posts are better than PDFs, which are better than videos or audio files.

Using a variety of media in different formats together, however, is the most powerful approach of all – a page linking to supporting blog posts, enriched with in-depth downloadable content, and brought to life with multimedia, is the ideal solution. But all of that takes time, effort and, most crucially, strategic planning.

The example diagram below shows the relative importance of each item of content with the service page at the centre of the spider web. Detailed, specific blog posts link there, conferring authority and driving traffic. In turn, social media links to those blog posts, putting them in front of their potential audience.

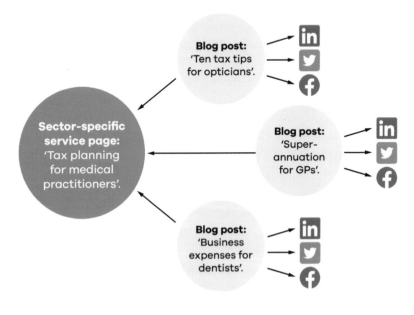

In practice, it's usually less tidy than that. You'll also want the blog posts to link to each other and might even want the service page to link back to certain high-value blog posts. Just remember that the page you most want to rank, in the highest position, is almost always going to be the service page.

Content planning

To build a content plan, you need two things: a blank calendar, and time and space to think. First, perhaps workshopping with colleagues, mark up fixed events in the year, such as:

- the self-assessment deadline
- the start of the new tax year
- seasonal events – religious holidays, school terms
- national or international events, eg International Women's Day
- events relevant to your clients, eg trade conferences
- local events – carnivals, festivals, sporting occasions.

That will already give you a sense of some beats you need to hit – 'Don't spend Christmas filling in your tax return' is a perennial classic suitable for blog posts or social media.

Next, set some communications priorities on a monthly or quarterly basis. For example, accountancy firms often experience acute client churn in February and March, so a priority might be lead generation, among one or more specific market segments, to rebuild the customer base. Similarly, quarter three, when things are often a little quieter because of summer holidays, might be a good time to focus on encouraging clients and prospects to research strategic decisions. A change in cloud accounting software, for example.

Finally, start filling in some specific items of communications – blog posts, social media posts, new pages on the website, webinars, and so on. As a bare minimum, for each piece of content, suggest a headline (you can always change it later) and give a brief outline of what you want it to say. This content calendar will form the centrepiece of your wider marketing plan.

A quick six-month content calendar

Time: 30 minutes

Alone or in a group, fill in the gaps in the following calendar by asking yourself the following questions:

- What's the most common question you're asked by clients?
- What's the funniest question you've ever been asked?
- What are allowable expenses for your buyer personas?
- What aspect of tax most surprises clients when you tell them?
- What should your personas do right now to make their lives easier?
- Why is your preferred cloud software the best for your clients?
- What was in the most recent fiscal statement from the Chancellor that will interest your buyer personas?
- What will Making Tax Digital mean for your clients in coming years?

Month	Content title	Summary
1		
2		
3		

Fig 8.1. Content calendar structure

Content marketing checklist

- ☐ Define content marketing goals
- ☐ Brainstorm content themes
- ☐ Longlist of content ideas
- ☐ Build a content calendar

Chapter 9

Build a marketing plan

In this chapter

You will learn:
What is a marketing plan? When to work on your plan. Managing and involving stakeholders. Structuring your plan. Scheduling and campaigns. *20 min read.*

A marketing **strategy** is a statement of what you want to achieve in the long-term; while a **marketing plan** sets out the specific, practical steps you're going to take to get there in the next six- or twelve-month period. It will probably overlap with your **content plan**, as discussed in the previous chapter, but should be wider-ranging and more comprehensive.

As an accountant, you're no doubt constantly trying to convince your clients of the need to budget, plan and forecast. The funny thing is, all the arguments they use also apply to marketing plans for accountancy firms.

We all know how pressed for time accountants are, and not every partner or director of an accountancy practice is willing to commit resources towards a marketing plan without having a guarantee of return on investment. A good marketing plan focuses time, energy and budget on what matters most, with business goals in mind. It maintains momentum and provides clarity about who needs to do what, by when, and why.

Medium-sized accountancy firms tend to recognise the value of coordinated marketing plans. They'll typically have an in-house marketer who builds plans around specific targets for the year, such as attracting a specific cohort of new clients, promoting services or simply reaching a wider audience.

For smaller firms, too, though – particularly those operating locally, competing against bigger rivals – a marketing plan combined with some creative use of content can be a cost-effective way to generate leads and help the practice grow.

The marketing plan should be a concrete document – something you've debated and discussed with key stakeholders, that they've signed up to, and that anchors marketing activity from that point on.

In practice, that probably means one or more of the following:

- a paper written in something like Microsoft Word
- a formal project plan using Gantt charts, swimlanes or similar
- a spreadsheet

Reviewing progress against the plan will ideally be a standing agenda item at team or board meetings, reminding everyone of the marketing goals and the contribution they have to make.

When to work on your marketing plan

It can be tricky to find the time to plan when you're focusing on the here and now. Timing your planning cycle correctly can help you to produce a marketing plan effectively and with minimum impact on the core of your role.

You might find that it's best for the planning cycle to coincide with or follow financial year-end so you can reflect on your marketing and financial objectives at the same time and make sure they match up.

If you need to get sign-off from partners or other stakeholders in your practice, make sure you factor this into your planning cycle. Make sure any deliverables are set out in a shared calendar or schedule. With a solid, comprehensive plan in place by, say, the end of April, maintaining it will be much easier. Schedule regular reviews and progress updates throughout the year.

Perhaps most importantly, your marketing efforts should complement your clients' priorities and activities. We at PracticeWeb would avoid contacting accountancy firms in January, for example, when you're drowning in tax returns. If you work with, say, potato farmers, you might want to avoid launching a campaign at the height of the harvest. Or if you work with tourism businesses, campaigns might be better timed for November than August.

Stakeholder management

Stakeholders are people who have something to gain from the success of your accountancy firm's marketing plan. Ideally, they'll not only help shape it but also offer support and guidance during its implementation.

First, though, you need to work out who owns your marketing plan and is ultimately responsible for its success. This will depend on a number of factors including the size of your accountancy practice and its level of commitment to marketing. Broadly speaking, we've identified three categories.

1. **Firms with an evolved marketing function.** If a practice has a marketing department, the chances are they've done this before, know what to do, and will be happy to own the plan and its KPIs.
2. **Those with limited marketing resources.** Where a practice has one person who is responsible for marketing, sometimes mixed with other duties, it might make sense for a partner to be the owner of the plan, even if they're not responsible for implementation.
3. **Practices with no marketing staff.** If nobody in your practice has overall responsibility for marketing, sharing the process between the firm's partners can work really well. In this situation, it's important to agree areas of responsibility and timelines upfront, including nominating one partner to be the ultimate owner.

Although it can be helpful to have creative minds in the room when drawing up a plan, it's not absolutely necessary for the owner to be a marketing person. They just need to know the business and its clients and, of course, be convinced of the value of marketing. You might then make up the rest of the marketing committee with partners and investors, or – a really smart move – more junior members of the team.

Other stakeholders might be key clients who, though you don't involve them directly in managing the marketing plan, you will want to have in mind when designing and reviewing it. You might consider getting their input informally through requests for feedback or just over a coffee if the opportunity arises.

Investors and lenders are also stakeholders and might ask to see your marketing plan before deciding to put more money into your firm to fund growth.

Structuring your marketing plan

It's useful to follow a set structure for this kind of business documentation because it makes it easier for stakeholders and investors to find the information they're looking for. A good marketing plan will include some or all of the following:

- SWOT analysis
- PESTLE analysis
- marketing goals
- growth areas
- capability assessment
- messaging
- tactics and schedule
- KPIs

Depending on the size and complexity of your accounting practice, you might need more or less detail in each of those areas.

A SWOT analysis is a useful tool for understanding your market position as it stands right now. Think specifically about the next period – are changes to the rules around off-payroll working going to affect your firm, for example? Are you planning an office move? What might be in the Spring Budget that your clients and prospects might want support in dealing with? The insight you gain here will be invaluable when it comes to identifying opportunities and avoiding problems. Look at each segment of your SWOT analysis independently. Talking to colleagues, clients and prospects can help ensure you have a complete and objective view of your situation.

If you feel that your business may need further detailed research into what external factors could affect and impact on its growth, then it may be worth carrying out a PESTLE analysis. This is a method for identifying and evaluating systematically the external factors that play a bigger role in shaping your company's sector of the market. It will give you a deeper understanding of possible threats to your business in the upcoming year and also in the marketing activity you may choose to invest in.

We talked about marketing goals in chapter four but, to reiterate, these should map to your business goals but with a clear marketing focus. They might centre on how you want your business to be perceived, how many leads you need to generate to meet your growth goal or the audiences you want to reach. Here are a few more examples:

- Get at least five client testimonials or reviews that mention the firm's expertise in offering business advice.
- Achieve 200 visits a month to the website through organic search.
- Increase traffic to the 'Accountants for the construction industry' page on the website by 50%.

Scheduling and campaigns

Finally, either as part of the content calendar discussed in chapter 6, or as a supplement to it, set out in specific detail:

- individual items of content that need to be produced
- who is responsible for producing them
- when they need to be delivered (leaving room for amends)
- when they'll be published
- which channels they'll go through.

If you plan to appear at industry shows or anchor marketing activities around key events such as the Spring Budget, you need to get planning and commissioning as soon as possible. If you're relying on colleagues to provide content, you'll want to make sure they know, have committed to doing it, and possibly even put it in their diaries.

Another way to think of your marketing plan is to break it down into a series of campaigns – phases of coordinated activity designed to hammer home specific messages. For example, if your vision is "to become the go-to fixed fee accountancy firm for taxi drivers" you might decide a key message is "We want cab drivers to feel rewarded for their hard work". That could translate into:

- a fortnightly blog post for two months
- a series of videos for Facebook
- an eBook called 'The complete guide to allowable expenses for cabbies'.

Alternatively, you might have one campaign running all year, tying together everything you do, or two long-term campaigns that dovetail and complement each other. The same rules apply, though – schedule everything, with named individuals responsible for delivery.

We've included a marketing plan template to help you get started and to populate with your own fields based on your marketing activity and plans. Download yours: https://bit.ly/3ALMCW7

Marketing plan checklist

- ☐ Review marketing goals and content plan
- ☐ Run marketing planning session with key stakeholders
- ☐ Share marketing plan as a concrete document
- ☐ Establish regular reviews

Measure success

Too often, people make decisions about marketing based on gut feeling and guesswork. That's a terrible shame because it's never been easier to monitor the performance of your marketing activity and make smart decisions based on hard data. You might say it's what digital marketing does best. In this chapter we'll be talking about what to measure (key performance indicators, or KPIs) and specific tools for measurement, including Google Analytics.

Marketing KPIs are specific metrics that your practice should be putting in place to measure progress against planned marketing activity. Historically, establishing KPIs for marketing was relatively more difficult than in some other areas. When accountancy firms advertised in local newspapers or put up billboards around town, they might observe an increase in enquiries. Other than that, though, how could you measure improvements in the perception of your brand? Nowadays, we've got all sorts of metrics to play with. Some of the popular key performance indicators against marketing channels include:

- **Marketing qualified leads (MQL)** – you need to be demonstrating that your sales revenue exceeds the cost of your marketing campaign.
- **Sales qualified leads (SQL)** – if a lead is accepted by your sales team, it is good to track the opportunity and if new business arises from it. On the other hand, if a lead is not accepted and you are getting a high ratio of poor leads, then you need to address why. For example, does the information you provide on your website fail to address what prospects are looking for? Is it hard to understand?

73

- **Cost per customer or per acquisition** – how much it costs you to acquire each new lead and the value of each of those leads. For example, attending an exhibition can be expensive for a company exhibiting but can also generate high quality leads because you have the right target audience in front of you and are able to screen them beforehand.
- **Social media reach** – knowing how many customers you are acquiring, and through which social media channels, you can more effectively focus your social media marketing.

By tracking specific marketing KPIs in weekly or monthly meetings you'll be able to reduce spend on activity which isn't working so well, and invest budget into areas where you are seeing significantly better results. Your marketing budget might be concentrated just on your website, or spent across multiple marketing channels such as social media, email marketing and digital advertising. In any case, each channel should have a clear return on investment (ROI) objective against it.

You can track multiple metrics but they all need to contribute to that aim of measuring change. For starters, a good metric should be comparative – you should be able to compare it to a different time period, client group, or traffic source. That will give you an understanding of which direction things are moving in. Being able to tell if you've had an increase in conversions since last month from a specific traffic source, for example, is more meaningful than just '2% conversion'.

A good metric should also be understandable. Keep things simple. Making metrics too complicated won't help you or others – you need to be able to explain it quickly and clearly and others need to be able to understand.

Finally, sound metrics will also drive change – in the way you run your marketing, in the behaviour of prospects on your site, in your own behaviour based on what the metric is telling you. For example, you might decide to do more social media advertising because the stats show it generates X more leads than other advertising, or spend less on paid media and put more effort into SEO because organic traffic converts more of the right types of clients.

To understand if your metrics are really effective ask if they're helping you...

- confidently enact change in your marketing
- make clear decisions on your marketing
- provide context for marketing activity
- know what's worked and what hasn't.

One particularly useful tool for tracking KPIs is a customer relationship management system (CRM). This will allow you to put leads that come via your website straight into a client database to which your team shares access. That makes it easier to manage future and current clients, systematise relationships through automated and segmented email marketing and power dashboard reporting.

Exercise

Define your first marketing KPI

Time: 20 minutes

- Use sticky notes or similar to brainstorm a long list of ideas of how you'll know your marketing programme is working.
- Review the list and separate out any that are easy to measure, such as average revenue per client (ARPC).
- Look at those which are hard to measure such as, say, brand awareness and pick one or two of the most important. Then think about whether there are proxies or secondary indicators that you could measure instead. For example, how many people are finding your website each month by Googling your brand name rather than by searching generic terms.
- Debate and vote: which KPI should become a standing item at management meetings?

Google Analytics

Google Analytics is an extremely powerful and free tool that Google offers to help you monitor and track your website traffic in more detail than you'll probably ever need. Through a simple bit of technology, a tracking code that sits invisibly on your website, it is able to present a dashboard showing who is visiting your site, where they're coming from and what they're doing while they're there.

As an accountant, you already know the value of data – and of turning it into actionable insights that inform your clients' strategic and tactical business decisions. You'll be working with various business intelligence tools, presenting analytical findings in reports, summaries, dashboards, graphs and charts to clients, providing intelligence about their business finances. Google Analytics does something similar only in this instance it's about assessing how well your marketing activity is performing in driving traffic to your website, what your visitors do once they land on your site and, most importantly, whether your website is converting traffic into enquiries and leads.

It doesn't take long to set up – you might already have it – and makes it possible to see how visitors are interacting with your website. What are they clicking on? Which other websites are they arriving from? And which pages do they dwell on, absorbing the content? All of this provides crucial insight to help shape your wider marketing and business strategy. As you become more familiar with Google Analytics, you'll be able to analyse the data it provides to assess return on investment. It's vital to be able to see which marketing activities are working, what needs changing and how marketing is driving commercial value for your firm.

The best way to approach Google Analytics is to first work out what you want to know and then interrogate the data. Here are a few of the key questions Google Analytics can help to answer:

- How many visitors am I getting to my website?
- Where is my website traffic coming from?
- What marketing tactics drive the most traffic to my website?
- Which pages on my website are the most popular?
- How many visitors have I converted into enquiries?
- What pages are converting traffic to enquiries?

- Where did my converting visitors come from and where on the website did they go?
- What blog content do my visitors like the most?
- Which parts of the country do my website visitors live in?
- What is the demographic breakdown of my visitors?

The Google Analytics dashboard provides information in several sections but there are three important ones you should focus on first.

First, the **audience overview** section provides details on traffic volume, engagement, demographics and user behaviour, giving a strong indication of whether you're driving substantial amounts of the right kind of traffic. The summary indicates quickly if you're attracting enough traffic to your site, how relevant the site might be and gives a high level temperature check on engagement. The users metric on the dashboard view gives you traffic volume. Changing the date range will help you assess how your marketing has performed in attracting traffic over a given period. Looking at pages, bounce rate and session duration tells us about the level of engagement of that traffic. You can then assess if you have a traffic problem, engagement issues, or both.

If your traffic sits below what you might expect, you need to take action to change that. Focusing on building volume before engagement and conversion is a sensible approach. If, on the other hand, you feel you have a healthy volume of traffic but your average bounce rate sits well over 50% and/or you see dwell times of less than a minute, you probably have an engagement or relevance problem. Users aren't hanging around – they don't like what they see – which means either the content or the audience is wrong.

You can dig deeper if you like, into **audience demographics**. Does the age and gender match my target client assumptions? Am I attracting the right type of prospects? Is our marketing reaching the right kinds of people? If you assume the majority of your clients are male and aged between 45-54 but Analytics is telling you your traffic is mostly female and aged 34-44, that's worth knowing.

A last point on audience: knowing where in the world your traffic is coming from, via the **audience location** section, is critical. You might find 40% of your traffic is coming from outside the UK and if you're only interested in marketing to UK businesses, you need to discount the rest of that traffic from your Google Analytics results.

Next, it's time to look at **acquisition**. This section will give you a good indication of whether you're persuading and attracting future customers through your marketing funnel. Under the acquisition section, you'll find information on different traffic sources, such as organic search, paid media, social media and people coming directly to your website by typing in the URL. This section is key to answering the question of where you are acquiring new visitors from, the level of engagement from each channel and, if you have goals set up, which channels convert most traffic.

Finally, the **behaviour** section will help you assess if your accounting firm's content marketing and key pages are performing in attracting prospects, their level of engagement with your content and, if you have goals set up, what's driving conversions. It uses two key metrics: page views and unique page views. This section will help you answer the following questions:

- What's the overall health of our content marketing activity?
- Are our key landing pages in the top 10 most visited?
- Did we have traffic spikes at certain times of the month or year?
- Which content created those spikes?

Knowing which pages attracted the most traffic and which had the most people exiting supports your marketing by indicating what to do more of, what to tweak and possibly what to stop doing. Typically you'll want to see your service pages and contact page in the top ten. If they're not, you need to work on driving traffic to those pages from off-site and better signposting from other pages on-site.

Measurement checklist

- ☐ Review vision and goals
- ☐ Set marketing KPIs
- ☐ Set up Google Analytics
- ☐ Establish regular checkpoints

Chapter 11

Review, maintain and refresh

In this chapter

You will learn:
Marketing as an ongoing process.
Marketing reviews – schedule and
structure. *15 min read.*

You should review your marketing strategy as part of your annual planning cycle. That will not only make sure it's still delivering return on investment but also refocus minds and give the process new energy. If you've followed the process set out in this book, you'll have a marketing strategy that's a multi-year process, not a one-off event, and you'll need those health checks and opportunities to change tack.

Your regular weekly or monthly marketing reviews are about monitoring progress against the plan. You might make some changes as you go based on emerging evidence but, ideally, you'd save big course changes for the annual review.

Most businesses schedule annual marketing reviews for December or January but, of course, that's not a great time for most accountancy firms with income tax self-assessment season underway. In fact, it doesn't really matter when the review takes place, as long as it's at about the same time each year. February might make sense, offering an opportunity to think about something other than tax returns and supporting your firm's efforts to generate leads as the new tax year approaches.

Give yourself at least half a day for some serious reflection and conversation. For a meaningful review, you'll want a year's worth of data to hand, including:

- marketing KPI reports
- annual website traffic statistics
- keyword rankings statistics
- social media engagement and follower numbers.

Were there particular items of content that continued to draw traffic long after they were initially posted and promoted? If so, that might influence your marketing plan for the year ahead. Are you seeing growth in your social media engagement? If not, you'll want to come up with a new approach – or perhaps simply post more often. Which themes, topics and content types seem to resonate most? You'll want to make sure the next year's plan includes more of that, and less of the other.

When it comes to reviewing your general approach, the easiest approach is to go back to chapter 1 of this book and go through the process again. Ask yourself at each stage if the decisions you made a year ago still hold up. In most cases, as long as the initial work you did was thoughtful and thorough, it will be about iterating rather than starting from scratch. For example, at PracticeWeb, we established buyer personas in 2018 which we decided to change towards the end of 2020 because two years' worth of data showed that, on balance, they weren't quite right. We changed one completely and tweaked the other two – test, learn, focus.

In light of changes to IR35, accountants whose personas included contractors a couple of years ago might be having similar thoughts. They might also be looking at the growth in the market for advice on research and development tax credits, and the burgeoning number of eCommerce businesses, and considering pivoting to a new niche.

You might also decide to undertake another round of market research and competitor analysis to test some new products and messages before making a decision. What's changed in the market, if anything? Are there more opportunities, or fewer? Is there more competition, or less? Has the attitude of potential clients shifted in important ways? If nothing else, 2020 saw a huge leap in digital capability and take up, for example.

When we reviewed our marketing strategy, we decided that our vision and values did stand up to scrutiny – they still resonated and felt right. And the time spent deciding that was a valuable opportunity to renew our collective understanding and commitment.

Marketing review checklist

- [ ] Set monthly review meetings covering
    - [ ] market research
    - [ ] buyer personas
    - [ ] vision
    - [ ] brand values and promises
- [ ] Amend marketing strategy documents
- [ ] Feed into annual marketing plan

Chapter 12

Conclusion

Marketing isn't just about winning business or pushing your services – it's about being in control of how you win that business and grow your firm.

It all adds up, from how you position yourself in the market to the specialisms you make a name for, meaning you can attract the clients you most want, at a pace that's right for you.

This manual contains all the information you need to put you firmly in control of growing a successful accounting firm through marketing.

More importantly, though, it provides you with a framework and a reference guide to refer back to as you grow your practice.

Use the techniques and methods in this book to understand your ideal clients, define your proposition and build your marketing strategy. You'll then have a roadmap for building your reputation, demonstrating your expertise and increasing your visibility.

We hope you're successful and that your accountancy practice thrives.

Keep in touch

We would love to hear how your journey is going. Connect with us on social media to start the conversation, and for the latest techniques, trends and insight around marketing for accountants.

You can also find more free marketing resources over on our website:

- Bite-size tips on our blog – practiceweb.co.uk/knowledge

- Beginners' guides – practiceweb.co.uk/knowledge/beginners-guides

- Complete marketing guides – practiceweb.co.uk/guides

- Research and data – practiceweb.co.uk/knowledge/insight

Writing style guide

Style refers to those elements of writing which do not necessarily have a universally agreed right or wrong answer. It covers details which might be handled differently from one newspaper to the next, and from one publishing house to another.

It matters because it adds consistency and polish and, in the subtlest of ways, underlines brand identity.

Your accountancy firm may already have its own style guidelines. If so, defer to those over the guidance given here. And where the guide below expresses no preference, we suggest referring to the AccountingWEB style guide or to a standard guide such as the *Oxford Style Manual.*

Acronyms and abbreviations

Do not use full points in abbreviations, or spaces between initials, including those in proper names: IMF, mph, eg, 6am, No 10, WH Smith, and so on.

As a general rule, use all capitals if an abbreviation is spoken out as individual letters (an initialism): BCC, UK, MTD, CGT, etc, but if it's an acronym (pronounced as a word) spell it out with initial capital, eg Radar, Laser.

Many accounting terms are marginal cases. For example, ISA, NICs and VAT can all be said as words but are pronounced as individual letters. Check the dictionary below if in doubt.

If there is any chance of ambiguity use all caps: LISA (lifetime individual savings account) rather than Lisa, for example.

Do not abbreviate inheritance tax as IHT.

Americanisms

Be wary of American spellings: 'centre', not 'center'; 'organisation', not 'organization'; and so on.

Ampersands

Only use if part of a trademark or recognised unit.

Apostrophes

Where the time period (two days) modifies a noun (time) – 'two days' time', 'two weeks' worth' and '12 years' jail'. Not 'three weeks old' or 'nine months pregnant', where the time period (three weeks) modifies an adjective (old). Test this by trying the singular: 'one day's time', but 'one month pregnant'.

The possessive in words and names ending in 'S' usually takes an apostrophe followed by a second 'S' (business's, boss's, James's), but be guided by how it sounds spoken aloud.

Bullet points

There are three ways of presenting bullets, as in the examples below.

List of items

Buckingham Ltd offers the following business services:

- audits
- bookkeeping
- cashflow forecasts

Bullets to break up a long sentence, in lieu of semicolons

Napoleon's defeat at Moscow is usually attributed to:

- the Russian policy of attrition
- dwindling supplies of food, ammunition and fuel
- the arrival of cold weather from the east.

Lists of complete sentences (recipes, processes, checklists, taxonomies)

There is only one way to make a good gimlet:

- Take a large saucer–style champagne glass.
- Add a jigger of dry gin, a teaspoon of simple syrup and half a teaspoon of lime cordial.
- Fill to the brim with chilled water (not carbonated).
- Add a single ice cube and a thin slice of lime.

Capitalisation

Don't capitalise ideas, schemes, projects or job titles merely because they seem Important, or their owners consider them so. (Material published by HMRC is often guilty of this.)

Capitalise ceremonial titles in specific cases, not in general.

Cap	Don't cap
Prime Minister William Gladstone	successive prime ministers
the Prime Minister	
Chancellor Randolph Churchill	chancellors of the 1980s
the Chancellor of the Exchequer said...	
the Chancellor yesterday announced...	
Captain W.E. Johns	rose to the rank of captain
the Government	government ministers
the Minister for Education	

Locations

'UK' or 'Britain', not 'United Kingdom' or 'Great Britain'. (Great Britain only includes England, Scotland and Wales.)

Treat regions as proper nouns and capitalise: 'South West' or 'West Midlands', not 'south-west' or 'west midlands'.

See also: **headlines.**

Cliches

In general, avoid well-worn figures of speech such as 'blast from the past', 'curate's egg' and 'all bets are off'. Look out for them during editing and either delete them or replace them with more original turns of phrase.

But cliches are a tough habit to kick (there's one) and they can be helpful in turning out a first draft. They also work well with certain brands as part of the tone of voice. Occasionally we might choose to employ a cliche for tactical reasons – 'death and taxes' is a handy way to lever the word 'death' into an article on inheritance tax for search engine optimisation purposes, for example.

Some pensions, tax and accounting specific cliches to avoid, if possible:

- bean counters
- burning a hole in your pocket
- death and taxes
- dip into your savings
- easing into retirement
- eggs in one basket
- golden years
- hand over fist
- in the money
- licence to print money
- made of money
- money doesn't grow on trees
- money to burn
- money where your mouth is
- nation of shopkeepers
- nest egg
- neither a borrower nor a lender be
- pennies
- pen-pushers
- piggybank
- twilight years

'The taxman' can be a useful synonym for HMRC, and is acceptable to use on occasions, but try to use 'the Revenue' instead.

Companies and organisations

Use names and spellings that companies and organisations use themselves, eg easyJet, eBay, iPhone.

Company names are always singular, not plural: "PracticeWeb offers its services", not "their services", and so on.

Dashes

Use a single en-dash as an alternative to a colon – like this. Use a pair of en dashes – in the middle of a sentence – instead of brackets. Don't confuse dashes with **hyphens**.

Dates

In prose and headlines write as, eg, 17 September 1964. Not:

- 17th September nineteen sixty-four
- 17th of September
- September 17
- September 17th
- 17/09/1964
- 17 Sept '64
- and so on.

When writing about ranges of years use 2021/22 for financial years, but 2021-22 in all other cases. If the range cuts across centuries write the years out in full: 1994-2014, not 1994-14.

Headlines and headings

Only capitalise the first word in a headline or heading. (Although fully-designed documents may break this rule for visual effect, depending on design trend at the time.)

Headlines should always be active over passive, eg 'HMRC confirms soft landing for MTD', not 'Soft landing confirmed for MTD'. In principle, 'A does B', not 'B is done'.

For digital copy, try to keep the headline under seven words, or around 55 characters.

For print copy, aim for no more than two decks (rows of text) with the bottom deck equal to or shorter than the top to lead the reader's eye into the story.

It is acceptable to use quotes in headlines, with single quotation marks, eg:

- BCC: 'Brexit is bad for business'
- Housing wealth 'will not solve housing crisis'

Follow the same rule when quoting headlines from other publications, with single quotation marks: 'Watchdog slams insurer over free pen offer', not WATCHDOG SLAMS INSURER OVER FREE PEN OFFER, or any other variation.

Hyphens

Use hyphens to join words or parts of words to avoid ambiguity.

Hyphenate compound expressions that are used before a noun to describe it, eg 'up-to-date guidance', 'basic-rate taxpayer', 'nil-rate band'. Expressions that follow the noun don't need hyphens: 'guidance that is up to date', 'a taxpayer at basic rate'.

Some phrases are always hyphenated, whether or not they precede a noun (year-end, year-on-year).

Hyphenate numbers when spelled out (thirty-five) and ages – a 35-year-old. (But no hyphens in '35 years old'.)

Also hyphenate five-year plan, four-monthly, a ten-foot shark, and so on.

Use a hyphen on the rare occasions things like the following crop up: 'to get the go-ahead', 'to say a big thank-you', 'to give the thumbs-up'.

Use hyphen when referring to age brackets, such as over-30s or under-21s (no apostrophe, lower case).

Don't confuse hyphens with **dashes**.

Income tax tables

There has been debate around how to record income tax thresholds, rates and bands in tables, with multiple approaches in common use.

Our style goes against the approach preferred by the UK Government, with figures laid out as in the following example, which offers the best combination of accuracy and clarity.

Personal allowance	Up to £12,500
Basic rate	Over £12,500 - £50,000
Higher rate	Over £50,000 - £150,000
Additional rate	Over £150,000

Italics

Do not use italics for emphasis – use bold.

Use italics for the titles of books, newspapers, films, albums, television programmes, and other substantial creative works:

- *the Guardian*
- *The Times*
- *The Telegraph*
- *Tomorrow's World*
- *Exile on Main Street*

Use single quotation marks for short stories, songs, poems, headlines and the titles of articles or blog posts.

Use italics for words or phrases in foreign languages, unless they have become naturalised and are commonly used in English. For example, italicise *bona vacantia* but not 'status quo' or 'faux pas'.

Job titles

Use lowercase for job titles, apart from political or ceremonial positions, eg 'Hall Pycroft, a stockbroker's clerk'.

For political positions, see **capitalisation.**

Numbers

In prose, write out numbers one to nine, and use numerals for 10 upward, even online.

Except, that is, in blog post titles: people are oddly more likely to click on '7 ways' than 'Seven ways'.

Be consistent within a sentence or clause: 'one in fifteen' or '1 in 15', never 'one in 15'.

On first mention, write £1.2 million and then £1.2m thereafter. The same applies for billions.

If it makes sense in context, write 'a hundred', 'five thousand', 'ten million', rather than using numerals.

Use numerals in tables and equations.

Use numerals for percentages, with a percent sign: 4%, not four per cent.

Avoid starting a sentence with a number: 'More than half (54%)...' is better than '54% said...'.

Use numerals with a forward slash for financial years: '2018/19', not '2018-19'.

See also: **hyphens.**

Organisations

See **Companies.**

Oxford Comma

This is the name given to a comma appearing before 'and' or 'but' in a list of three or more items, otherwise known as a serial comma. Our approach is pragmatic: avoid serial commas in general, and consider restructuring lists to sidestep the issue altogether.

Example "Famous writing style guides include those by Fowler, Strunk and White, and Gowers" is better as "Famous writing style guides include those by Strunk and White, Fowler and Gowers", with no serial comma required.

But if after all that if including an Oxford comma truly makes a sentence clearer, more elegant or just more stylish, go for it.

No serial comma:
- salary, dividends, interest, rent or loans
- strengths, weaknesses, opportunities and threats

Serial comma:
- 'fish and chips, ham and eggs, and coronation chicken sandwiches' (where multiple list items are units containing 'and')
- 'vehicles, office equipment, property, and so on' (preceding catch–all extension)
- 'a chocolate egg, a surprise, and a toy' (emphasis, clarity).

Quotations

Follow newspaper style:

- Double quotation marks when reporting something a particular person said or wrote in a particular place, at a particular time.
- Single marks for nested quotations.
- Wrap a quotation mark inside the full stop when paraphrasing. For example, Speaking at Accounting Excellence, our editor said "I like listicles".

Example: "When he shouted, 'Lend me your spectacles' I was astonished," said Sir Hilary, "and I'm afraid to say they were never returned."

Single quotation marks, AKA inverted commas, can also be used for distancing, explanation or to add clarity, eg "He advised 'writing-down allowances' as the client had already claimed the annual investment allowance."

Sentences beginning with 'and' or 'but'

"There used to be an idea that it was inelegant to begin a sentence with and. The idea is now dead." – Sir Ernest Gowers, *The Complete Plain Words*, 1954

Whatever you were taught at school, you should feel free to begin sentences with and or but. It can help break up long sentences, which is especially useful online, and conveys modernity in prose. But don't do it too often or it can become annoying.

Trademarks

Tread carefully for legal reasons: the rule of thumb is to use generic alternatives unless there's a good reason not to, ie 'ballpoint pen' over 'biro' (but if it really is a Biro – capitalise it).

Most trademarks are generally capitalised, ie Tarmac. It's a company and should be capitalised; the road surfaces we walk and drive on are generally made of asphalt.

The only exceptions should be where a company itself capitalises in unorthodox ways, ie 'iPhone'. This is done as those who own the trademark can sue for misuse, although this rarely happens in practice.

Dictionary

adviser – not advisor, unless it is part of the name of a firm which spells it that way.

annual pension allowance – singular, not plural.

auto-enrolment – *noun* – hyphenated.

bookkeeper/bookkeeping – one word, no hyphen.

business's – apostrophe followed by 's'.

bounce-back loan – *noun*, lower case, hyphen.

cashflow – one word, no hyphen.

Chancellor – capitalised when used as a title, eg Chancellor Randolph Churchill.

childcare – one word.

CO_2 – *noun*, write as a formula.

coronavirus – *noun*, not capped, one word.

cost-effective – hyphenated.

COVID-19 – *noun*, capped and hyphenated, a coronavirus disease. The coronavirus is also acceptable.

cybercrime, cybersecurity, cyber-attack – usually one word

eBook – *noun*. Time-sensitive and will evolve to 'ebooks' in future. Monitor this.

eCommerce – *noun*. May evolve in future.

email – *noun and verb*. Usage evolved over the course of decades.

first–time buyer – hyphenated.

focused – not focussed.

government – lower case in all instances unless referring to 'the Government'.

General Election – cap in the lead-up to an election, eg 'General Election 2019'. Down cap 'general election in 2017'.

Help-to-buy – lower case and hyphenated.

High net-worth – hyphenated.

letting relief – not 'lettings relief'.

licence – *noun* – 'driving licence'.

license – *verb* – 'licensed to drive'.

Marketeer – *noun* – not 'marketer'

Making Tax Digital – capitalised, spelled out on first use; thereafter, MTD.

Minister – capitalised as part of a specific title, eg Minister for Education; lower case for the plural and in general: "When she became a government minister...".

no one – two words; not 'no-one' or 'noone'.

Parliament – *noun* – cap when referring to 'the Parliament', downcap other mentions.

practice – *noun* – 'accounting practice'.

practise – *verb* – 'practising accountant'.

Prime Minister – capitalised as a title, eg Prime Minister William Gladstone, or with reference to the current incumbent – the Prime Minister. Lower case in general.

remuneration – *noun* – not 'renumeration'.

revaluate – *verb* – "not re-evaluate". Commonly used with business rates.

round-up – *noun* – hyphenated: 'this round–up of facts and figures'.

round up – *verb* – two words: 'in which we round up all the facts and figures'.

National Insurance – capitalised, lower case the various classes with numeral.

Number 10 (Downing Street) – *proper noun* – capitalised, digits.

self–assessment – *noun* – hyphenated.

startup – *noun* – one word: 'business startup'.

start–up – *adjective* – hyphenated: 'start-up business'.

start up – *verb* – 'to start up the engine'.

subcontractor – one word.

taxpayer – *noun* – one word. Hyphenate: 'basic-rate taxpayer', 'higher-rate taxpayer' and 'additional-rate taxpayer'.

think tank – *noun* – two words.

write-off – *noun* – hyphenated: 'it's a write-off'.

write off – *verb* – two words: 'to write off'.

writing-down allowances (WDAs) – hyphenated; use abbreviation after first instance in text.

Social media best practice

The major social media providers are constantly tweaking their algorithms and staying on top of what works is a full-time job. This handy reference covers the basics.

Hashtags

Across most social media platforms, hashtags are a useful tool for reaching people who aren't following you or connected. For example, if you specialise in working with charities, you might want to add #UKCharity to relevant posts.

Don't overload your posts with hashtags, though, or they risk looking like spam and irritating those who come across them.

Using sentence case (#SocialMediaTips) rather than all lower-case (#socialmediatips) not only makes hashtags easier to read but also makes them more accessible to people using screen readers.

Images

On Twitter and Facebook, posts with images tend to get better engagement than those without. On LinkedIn, that isn't always the case – text-only posts often perform well – so try posting with and without to see what works for you. Instagram is, of course, all about images.

Video

On Facebook, video performs better than any other media type. Video also works well across other platforms, as part of your overall mix of content. Videos don't have to be slick or professional – immediacy and personality is more important. Newer platforms such as TikTok focus solely on video and some accountants are already making good use of them to connect with particular audiences.

Twitter

Header image size	1500 pixels x 500 pixels (3:1)
Profile photo size	400 x 400 (1:1)
Tweet image size	1024 x 512 (2:1)
Maximum hashtags	Two
Advice	Twitter is a great way to drive traffic to your website – make sure you post links to all your blog posts, ideally more than once. Also consider sharing condensed versions of your blog posts as threads – chains of Tweets linked together. This is a great way of maintaining the visibility of your content over hours. Don't just broadcast – who you follow, favourite and Retweet is important, too. Connect with your clients and any bodies or publications in your chosen specialist sectors and engage with their Tweets.

LinkedIn

Header image size	1584 x 396 (4:1)
Profile photo size	400 x 400 (1:1)
Post image size	1200 x 627
Maximum hashtags	Three
Other notes	By default, LinkedIn presents a custom version of the feed to each user based on which content they've previously liked or engaged with. In general, aim for a mix of text, video and image-based content and then tailor your approach based on what gets the best engagement from your connections. LinkedIn users are more likely to connect with individuals than to follow company accounts so get your partners active on the platform, too.

Facebook

Cover photo size	851 x 315
Profile photo size	400 x 400 (1:1)
Post image size	1200 x 630 (1.91:1)
Maximum hashtags	Four
Other notes	Facebook is especially good for making local connections and for reaching businesses with a local focus.
	Changes to the algorithm in recent years have made it harder to reach audiences without paying to promote posts but it's still worth posting.
	You'll certainly want to make sure your business listing is accurate, up to date and complete.

Instagram

Profile photo size	320 x 320 (1:1)
Post image size	Instagram automatically resizes and crops but make sure you upload an image of at least 1080 x 1080.
Maximum hashtags	30
Other notes	The biggest challenge for accountants is knowing what to post on Instagram. Using Canva or Adobe Spark you can create animated explainers, tips or quotes, just using graphics and text. Instagram made its name with selfies – don't be afraid to show your face. This can be a great way to establish informality and make connections. Consider posting photos of client businesses. If you work with a lot of cafes, for example, there's plenty of opportunity for visual appeal there.

Digital marketing glossary

When you're a specialist, it's easy to forget that the words, phrases and jargon you use every day aren't universally understood. This was brought home to us when a client asked us to explain (a) what SEO means and (b) what a blog is. This glossary is intended to help those who, though they might be expert accountants, don't know much about marketing or communications. Some of it you'll already know, other bits you might have *thought* you knew and some, we hope, will answer questions you've been too embarrassed to ask.

Architecture | How the information on your website is structured, including hierarchy and connections. It may or may not be reflected in the site navigation.

AdWords | The previous name for *Google Ads*, Google's online pay-per-click advertising platform.

Back-end | The settings, code and technology that lie behind *user interfaces*, usually invisible to end users.

Blog | Short for 'web log'. Blogs (noun) are run by bloggers who engage in blogging (verb). A blog is a regularly updated stream of topical content and commentary – anything from a personal diary to a company information feed.

Blog post | An individual entry on a blog. An article, essentially.

Bounce rate | The volume of visitors to your website that navigate away after viewing only one page – that bounce straight off.

Brand | The unique personality and values of a business expressed through, and informing the development of, written content, web design, graphics and so on.

Buyer journey | The steps a potential customer or client goes through before making the final decision to sign up for goods or services.

Campaign Monitor | One of the main email marketing platforms used by businesses to manage client newsletters and email campaigns. See also: *MailChimp*.

Canonical link | To avoid *duplicate content* where the same material appears on more than one website, or more than once on the same website, it is possible to specify in the *back-end* which version you'd prefer search engines to index.

Clickbait | A post or article with a deliberately provocative or intriguing title designed to encourage users to click through. Rarely used on accountancy websites.

Click-through-rate (CTR) | A ratio expressing how often those who see your ads online end up clicking on them, used to assess the performance of ads and keywords. It equates to the number of clicks your ad receives divided by the number of times your ad is shown.

Content | Words, images, eBooks, video and anything else that makes up the substance of your website.

Conversions | When people respond to your marketing by undertaking a specific action such as emailing or phoning to enquire about your services.

Conversion rate optimisation (CRO) | The practice of making systematic changes to a website to increase the number of conversions.

CTA | Call to action – an instruction given to website users indicating what you want them to do next. "Pick up the phone now" is a typical CTA.

CTR | See *click-through rate*.

DNS | Domain name system. A global system for identifying computers, services and anything else connected to the Internet used, most importantly, to ensure that when users enter an easy-to-remember website address such as practiceweb.co.uk, they get taken to the right place.

Display advertising | Paid-for adverts that appear on commercial websites, typically in the form of banners at the top of the page or breaking up the content.

Duplicate content | Material that appears in exactly the same form on more than one website, or on multiple pages on the same website. As long as only one version is *indexed*, or a *canonical link* has been specified, it's not necessarily bad news but otherwise can seriously damage your *search ranking*.

GIF | An image file format designed to reduce file size for use online. Most often used for graphics, logos and illustrations rather than photographs. GIFs can also be animated which has made them popular on social media. Pronunciation is highly controversial but we prefer 'giff' to 'jiff'.

Google Ads | Google's online pay-per-click advertising platform which delivers paid-for results alongside *organic search results*.

Google My Business | Google's free directory that plays a key role in your business's online listing.

Google penalty | Certain practices or attributes can prompt Google to penalise your website, pushing it far down the search results or removing it from the index altogether.

House style | A technical aspect of *branding* governing the specific details of writing – should you start sentences with 'and' or 'but'? Does your firm spell it 'cash flow' or 'cashflow'?

Horizon | PracticeWeb's platform for building websites.

HTML | Hypertext markup language. It uses *tags* to define how content displays on a web page.

HTML title | Text defined with the title tag in *HTML* will show in your web browser's title bar or the name of a tab. Title tags also define what will be displayed in search engine results as the headline which people click on to visit the page. HTML titles are important for *SEO*.

Index | Search engines such as Google maintain a vast map of all the pages they scan, rank and might potentially return in search listings. Website owners can request that certain pages be *no-indexed*.

Internal links | Links that go from one page to another page on your website.

JPG | Or Jpeg, pronounced Jay-peg. An image format that uses an algorithm to remove unnecessary detail to reduce the file size. Most photographs you view online will be in JPG format.

Keywords | Ideas or topics that define what your content is about.

Landing page | A special page set up to serve a particular marketing campaign, allowing easy tracking of the effectiveness of, say, pay-per-click advertising, and the measurement of return on investment.

Lead-gen | Lead generation, a common objective for accountancy websites.

Listicle | An item of content in the form of a list, eg 'The 27 top Xero hacks that will revolutionise your life'. (Often also *clickbait*.)

Long-form content | Articles or blogs of substantial length – at least 1,000 words, ideally more – on which Google places particular value.

MailChimp | One of the world's biggest email marketing platforms used by many businesses to design and manage newsletters and campaigns. See also: *Campaign Monitor*.

Metadata | Information about what a given web page includes and covers that, among other functions, helps search engine algorithms work out how to classify and rank your website.

Meta description | A short snippet of around 155 characters summarising the contents of a web page, included as an HTML tag but not visible on the page to users. It may be used by search engines in displaying results.

Mobile-first indexing | This refers to Google's general practice of looking at the mobile version of a web page rather than the one that displays on desktop PCs. If your page doesn't render well on mobile devices, it may not rank well, regardless of how good it looks on desktop machines.

Mobile-responsive | Websites that are specifically designed for smartphones or tablets.

Newsfeed | Superficially similar to a blog but with a focus on factual information. PracticeWeb supplies many clients with a flow of daily news stories which appear in the newsfeed on their websites. Because it's generic, this content is *no-indexed*.

No-index | Content which is viewable on your website but which is not included in a search engine's *index*. There's no way to guarantee a page won't be indexed but you can include a request to 'no-index' in the code for your website. You might want to do this if, for example, a page duplicates content from elsewhere on your site which might otherwise hurt your search engine ranking.

Organic search results | Google returns two types of results in response to searches: ads and organic results. The latter have ranked because of their inherent qualities as assessed by Google search algorithms.

Organic traffic | Visits to your website by people who have found it through *organic search results*.

Persona | Buyer personas, or user personas, are a way of thinking about target clients that makes strategic decision making easier, by prompting you to focus on a specific imaginary user, not a broad demographic.

Podcast | Content in audio format, like a radio programme but available to download and listen to at any time. Podcasts have been around since the mid-oos but really took off in the past five years. Our sister business, AccountingWEB, has a weekly podcast called *No Accounting for Taste*.

PNG | An image format used to reduce the size of files for use online. Most commonly used for graphics, logos and illustrations, rather than photographs. Similar to *GIF* but generally considered superior.

PPC | 'Pay Per Click' is a model of internet marketing in which advertisers pay a fee each time one of their ads is clicked.

SEO | 'Search engine optimisation' is the practice of tweaking content and website settings to encourage Google to present your website higher in search results.

SERP | Search engine results page. What you see in response to a query entered into Google.

Social media | Facebook, Twitter and LinkedIn are all examples of social media, designed to facilitate fast, informal sharing of media with followers or friends.

Tags | HTML tags define how your web browser should format and display the content but are not shown to users. These days, most people edit using *WYSIWYG* and never have to use tags. Tags are also used to contain *metadata*.

Tone of voice | How you want to address your audience online. An aspect of *branding* relating to *house style*.

Unindexed | See *no-index*.

UX | User experience – how a user feels, reacts and behaves while using a website.

Values | Statements that summarise neatly what a business or *brand* is about and act as an anchor for any marketing activity, even if they're never stated outright.

White-label content | Content that is produced by PracticeWeb that you then pay for and use under your practice's name or brand.

WordPress | A content management system designed initially for blogging but now used to power all sorts of websites. Our product *Horizon* is built on WordPress.

WYSIWYG | 'What you see is what you get'. A type of editing software in which the content reflects the appearance of the finished product.

PracticeWeb